Still Half Full

Alexis Diaz

ACKNOWLEDGMENTS

A special thanks to my family and my close friends who didn't hesitate to support me from the moment I opened up and said aloud that I needed help.

Without the endless encouragement and reassurance from all of you, I wouldn't have had the space or confidence to create this book.

Thank you.
Love, Alexis

Instagram: @alexiswrotethat

INTRODUCTION

This book is a collection of random thoughts and short poems I wrote through a period of my life that consisted of immense heartache and constant inner healing. The very first poem was written in the first apartment I shared with my ex-partner of seven years. After one of our very frequent middle of the night arguments, I sat on our couch crying, feeling very alone, lost, and empty. I didn't know how to cope, so I wrote. Writing gave me an outlet to release my thoughts and my emotions without filter nor judgement. By writing down my thoughts and emotions as I was feeling them, I got to understand and reflect on my own pain and heal in my own time, at my own pace. I didn't know it at the time, but this was the beginning of me releasing the pain and guilt and refilling myself with love, confidence, power, and peace.

Why

Why do women yell?
It's because we are never heard even when someone
is listening

Why do women yell?
It's because we have a heart full of passion, ready to
explode,
And when we love,
We love hard

Why do women yell?
It's because we often feel so alone in a crowded room
And no one seems to hear us.

Fight

Do we fight with passion
Or with poison?

Do we fight with our hearts
Or with our heads?

Do we fight for one another
Or against each other?

Do we fight to uplift
Or to belittle?

Do we fight
Or do we flee?

Code Word

When you say, "I love you," is it code for? . . .

I am scared to be alone

I am afraid to start over

You are merely a place holder in my life

You are "good enough" for right now

Or is it code for? . . .

You chose me

You never want to lose me

I am your forever

Please . . .

What is it that you really mean?

Comfort vs Anguish

Comfort

The feelings you give me aren't like any I've felt
before—

They make me feel so full of life
So grateful to have met you
So comforted by the thought of being yours

The good outweighs the bad on any given day
Our love blossoming like a flower in May
Laughing, loving, and living life solely with and for
one another

I want to feel these feelings forever

Comfort vs Anguish (cont.)

Anguish

The feelings you give me aren't like any I've felt
before—

They make me feel so empty
So invisible
So uncomfortable with the thought of being yours

The bad outweighs it all
Our love is cold, angry, grey
Going through the motions without and against one
another

I never want to feel these feelings again.

Insecurities hurt

Your insecurities held me at my throat

Any move I made; their grip grew tighter

They fiddled a cacophony of sound with my emotions

Playing the same tune

Suddenly, silence . . .

Wind chimes, chime in the distance

Your insecurities slip away to rest

You fiddle a dulcet melody with my wounded emotions

Playing my favorite song

Only for a few seconds long.

Reminder #1

You may feel broken

But you remain whole

You may feel empty

But you are still full.

No Synergy

When she is in love, his energy is her energy

However, his energy doesn't coincide with her energy

No, it consumes it

It shifts the air in the room from ease to stiffness

Her energy depleting without a thought in her mind

Without her control

Regardless of the energy draining from within her

His energy, now and forever, will dictate the mood of the room.

Love I

Love is a crazy thing

People tell you love is beautiful, which indeed it is

But they forget to tell you that it's only beautiful
when
It's the right kind of love—

The love that is understanding and compassionate

The love that makes you feel complete

The love that you feel in your heart
And in every breath you take

The right kind of love is wild and free—

So much more beautiful than the eyes can see.

Love II

Love is addicting

With each embrace you fall deeper into bliss

After every bad fight, you yearn for that first hit
Of love followed by lust

That first high—

The high of being in love, being lifted into ecstasy

The high of feeling completely content
Filling with upmost peace

That high is unbearably good

That high is addicting.

Love III

Love is . . .

When you're together and nothing feels more right

When you fall deeper in love with every synchronized inhale

And your head reaches the clouds with each exhale

The energy between us filled the entire room with love

Love isn't just an emotion or an explanation

Love is an energy that cannot even be defined by a singular word or feeling

Love is unexplainable.

What to do . . .

What to do when I am stuck between a rock
And a hard place

What to do when I want to listen to my heart,
But I know I should listen to my head

What to do when life pulls me in one direction,
But the wind takes me in another

What to do when the person I can't live without
Is the person I need to let go.

Nothing

I've loved so hard
I've begged so loud
I've cried so much

That now I feel nothing

Your words used to cut so deeply
They would lacerate my heart and
Shred through my thoughts; constantly replaying

Your words now empty
With no meaning left
They no longer linger

Yet, I still feel nothing.

Second Chances

How many "second chances" are there?

Is there a limit?

Is it still a "second chance" the third time?

Is "second chance" a synonym for "I'm sorry"?

Perhaps second chances are infinite in your universe.

No Name

What is that feeling that pulls you back to someone
That you know isn't good for you?

Is it even a feeling?

Does it have a name?

Is it a condition?

Or do we run back out of guilt?

Out of love?

Out of the fear of being alone?

Identify yourself, no name.

Random Thoughts

Many people don't believe in love,
in soulmates or in the infamous phrase "the one"

But when I saw you from across the room,
One summer night, at a party

I had never felt a feeling so moving, so real
It compelled me to meet you
To speak to you
To get to know you by any means necessary

Before that moment, no one had made me feel even
remotely Close to the feeling I experienced that night

I had never wanted to give my heart, body, mind and
soul to someone so bad

From that night on I was a believer in love, soulmates,
"the one".

Is it really love? . . .

If you love me why does hurting me come so easy?

Why do you choose to pit us against each other?
Why do you choose to disrespect me?
Why do you shut me out?

Yet when I try to walk away . . .

You bring up the good times
The memories
Our history

You try to convince me that the good trumps the bad

But you fail to realize you've never apologized
You've never acknowledged the bad

Do you even really love me?

A Good Night's Rest

You leave me
Say that you need me

You break me
Say that I'm crazy

You say I am no good for you
Say you can't live without me

Say you have to let me go while you hold open the
door
Waiting for me to be the one to walk out
Carrying all of your pain
All of the blame

Just so you can sleep at night
Just so you can justify the damage you've done.

Betrayal

You accused me of betrayal

Insisted I exploited our privacy

Convinced I was cheating

Not really sure why

I used to defend my name like I was in a court of law

Eventually I gave up
Let you rant
Let you believe whatever make-believe story it was
that day

In reality, you betrayed me
You betrayed our love
Our respect
Our relationship—
You betrayed us.

Lovesick

Your love has me bedridden
Holding my inhibitions in the pit of my stomach
My body aches for your affection

I threw up my self-worth onto the floor
Sweating bullets of shame
Coughing up my sensibility

Wishing I could go back to a time I felt better.

Bittersweet Relief

I cried for so long

And as the tears became less and less
I felt relieved—

Relieved, that I no longer wanted the heartache
Relieved, that I was strong enough to leave
Relieved that I left

Although I feel as if a weight has been lifted,
I still cry

Not because I'm sad
Not because I miss you

Because I missed me.

Growth

When there isn't anyone to tell you
How pretty you look today—
To make you smile when you're sad
Tell you everything is going to be ok
When you are having a bad day

When it's just you—

YOU have to be the one to tell yourself "you look
pretty today"
YOU have to be the one to make yourself laugh and
smile
YOU have to remind yourself that everything is
going to be ok

That is growth.

Thoughts

Sometimes I think to myself . . .

How do I love again?
I've already experienced a love so strong
A love filled with passion, excitement, loyalty and
love

As I look back, I realize that wasn't love
But it also wasn't not love
I'm actually not sure what to call it

I like to think we loved each other
Perhaps more than we loved ourselves
Dependent on each other for so much

And so, through the years I lost myself to you
In the unspoken race of power and control

Trying to love ourselves
Competing with the love, we had for one another

Although our love was so strong as a whole,
We were lacking so much individually

I eventually began to win myself back
Find my voice, my path, myself.

Unsolicited Questions

After a breakup, expect—
The prolonged
Dragged out
High pitched
"What happened?"

Followed by the deeply concerned melodramatic
"Are you okay?"

"What happened," you ask?

How do you explain what happened
When you can't even explain it yourself?

When point A to point Z had too many bumps in
the road

To even begin to explain, better yet in a couple of
sentences

When the problems became such a cluster fuck
And you can't even remember where or when they
started

I can't even explain it to myself

So how can I possibly begin to explain it to someone
else?

Sometimes I wish it was as easy as cheating,
Falling out of love, or moving on
But unfortunately, it was so much more complicated
than that.

Unsolicited Questions (cont.)

"Am I okay," you ask?

The short answer is, "I'm great, never been better"
And the truth is—I am great
I have never felt better.

But I'm also sad
Sometimes lost

I'm adjusting to being alone
Enjoying my own company
Finding myself again
Focusing on myself

Reading a book
Picking up new hobbies
Revisiting old hobbies
Reconnecting with past connections
Making new relationships

The only answer is, "I will be ok."

Confused

What is it that I'm feeling?

I don't know what I'm feeling

I have a million memories and thoughts
Running through my mind
Burning a hole in my heart

Yet my mind feels blank
My heart feels empty

I can't seem to find the right words to explain it all.

What exactly do I miss? . . .

I miss you every day, some days more than others
I miss our love, today especially
I miss your embrace, your kisses, your warmth

Together, I felt on top of the world
Certainly, we would be the ones to make it to forever

When we kissed, I feened for more, longing for the
next one
I never once grew tired of them; I still think of them
constantly

I would do anything for one more kiss
One more embrace
One more moment in time
You're holding me, tightly yet ever so gently
That it felt like home

I would feel the love flowing within us,
Between us and all around us
It would take over my body
It felt better than any high
I would smile from ear to ear,
Questioning how I ever got so lucky

I miss you

No—
I miss our love
I miss the good times
I miss the high
Not you.

Individuals

At age 16, I knew I loved you

I knew I didn't want anyone else but you

In fact, I didn't plan for anyone else but you

In my eyes our love was perfect
We were perfect
A dream team

It was everything I could have dreamed of and more

It felt as if we were made for each other

Over time, then all at once, everything went wrong

My life was turned upside down right in front of my
eyes

Now I am suddenly planning my life without you in it

Planning it only for me, trying to see where
Someone else, anyone else, will fit
I wasn't ready for all of this
I never prepared for any of this

I was so sure about us

But I guess life, or the universe, had its own plans for
us

As individuals.

Grieving process

Are you supposed to grieve after a breakup?

The process feels very similar

I feel myself going through the stages of grief

Some days I couldn't be happier and content

Other days I miss you, miss what we had

Some days I replay the good times in my head,
Wishing I could relive them one more time

Other days I feel guilty for walking out on you
And shutting you out so harshly

Some days I love myself for finally choosing me
And leaving you behind

Other days I pray for you and your family

Some days I don't think about you at all

Other days I break down and cry, yearning for our
love

Most days I accept that is my new normal.

Confessions

I have to learn how to love again

Open up and be vulnerable again

I have to learn how to be intimate with someone new

Learn to be infatuated with someone else

This is hard for me

I need more time to adjust and process

I feel as though I haven't fully processed my feelings
Or my new reality

Who do I blame for this?

Low Points

I feel empty

I feel numb

I felt so much love for so long

Now it's gone

All I feel is nothing

I want to feel

Something

Anything.

Lie down with me

When I go to lie down with a man,
I am yearning for intimacy

When I go to wrap my legs around him
And push my chest into his,
I am dying to melt into him

But when I am laying down with a man,
I am nothing more than an empty vessel

My eyes are full of sweet nothings

My embrace is cold

My mind wonders and
I crave to be alone again.

Energy Vampire

She was so full of love
She radiated positive energy
She had enough spirit to fill up a room

He was full of doubt
He oozed negative thoughts
He had enough insecurities to fill up an auditorium

She desired to teach him love and acceptance
He desired to drain her

She had plenty to spare, but only for so long
He thought he had forever to consume her.

Morning Reflections

Some mornings I wake up thinking about
The could haves and the should haves—

I should have been more empathetic
I should have compromised more
I should have tried harder to understand you
I should have tried to help you more

I shouldn't have left you.

Guilty Conscience

For a long time, I felt so much guilt
For even thinking of leaving you
Guilty for wanting to love myself more than I loved
us
Guilty for possibly abandoning you when you needed
me most

This guilt chipped away at my spirit
Transformed me into a different person
I let go of the best parts of me for you
I gave up my happiness and myself,
Trying to help you find yourself

You let me feel guilt
Watched the best parts of me diminish
Stripped me of the very things that made me who I
am
Fed the guilt and didn't blink twice.

Wishful Thinking

I wish I could talk to you

Tell you how much I miss you

That I still love you, whole heartedly

That even though I act like I'm ok,
I still think about you

It hurts

Pains me that I can't tell you

Afraid if I open up and let you in again,
I won't be able to let you go.

And I have to let go
For you. For me. For our sanity

We have to accept it

We weren't soulmates

You were just this chapter's love story.

Bittersweet Memories

Once the pain subsides

Saudade rushes over me

All I can think about are the good times

The infinite amount of time we thought we had with

each other

How we went from absolutely in love to enemies
These thoughts invade my brain
Like cancer spreading and multiplying every second

Part of me doesn't want them to leave

All of me will indulge

Reliving these moments for as long as I can

The reminder hurts so good.

Fortune Teller

What does the future hold?

How do you know what's right or wrong?
How do I differentiate between if we are meant

To be or not to be?

If I'm still in love with you?

If I'm just lonely?
I fear that I love love so much that
I am yearning for that feeling of being in love and
not you.

Reminder #2

That wasn't love
You told me you were unsure of us
Unsure of me
That you could do better

I didn't deserve that
I deserve better
I am worth better.

Past Hurt

You doubted my love

Questioned my intentions

Battered my compassion

Buried my light

But . . .

I won't let this define me

I will heal.

Serious Talks

Being in another serious relationship frightens me

Possibly falling in love again, only to experience all
the agony That comes with it scares me

As much as I love,
Love can be scary

When any man gets remotely serious
I want to run and never look back

Yet I crave being in love

What exactly am I missing?

When will I feel comfortable having serious interac-
tions?

When will I feel ready to accept love again?

Reruns

For a split second I think about trying again
Starting all over with a clean slate
Pretending we are strangers, meeting for the first
time

Just to see if we can get it right this time
To know for sure if we are truly meant to be together.

Misdesign

To be aware but be naive ...
Is it a flaw in our design?
Is it in our human nature to ignore the signs?

Does our heart love the pain so much
It numbs the brain,
Silencing our logic reasoning?

So we can go on receiving the pain
Remaining "unaware".

Prayers

I pray for you

I pray you find peace

I pray that you're being kind to yourself

I pray you reach your full potential

I pray you become the man you always pictured you would be

I pray you fall in love with yourself

I pray for you.

Self-Reflection

I think of certain instances
Replaying past situations
Outside looking in, thinking about how I could have
revised What I said
I realize only now that I played the blame game too
This doesn't excuse the behavior demonstrated
But I wasn't perfect either

I had flaws
I have flaws

Being alone, physically and mentally
Left me to reflect on the worst parts of me
Being surrounded by family and friends
Not by the person you lie down with every night,
Opened my eyes.

I am selfish
I am inconsiderate
I am so free spirited that when the wind moves, I
move
Before stopping to look around to see
Who is still beside me

I shut people out
I rarely let people in
I show them all the good and only sometimes the
bad

I have flaws too.

Say It With Me

Always open
Always flowing
Always growing.

Myths

They say to get over someone you should get under another

However, that doesn't really work, does it?

It's more of a distraction than a solution,

A temporary fix to an ever-breaking heart

Because how do you replace someone who is irre-placeable?

How do I get over the person I love,
With a person I don't even know?

Reminder #3

Treat yourself how you expect others to treat you.

Dear Mom

I refrained from opening up
Sparing you from my despair

Realistically sparing my own embarrassment
I was ashamed
I was supposed to be—
Your confident, strong, independent daughter

How could I tell you I was failing?
Failing to be the woman you raised me to be
A fraud to my own upbringing
I knew I wasn't being true to my name
I stayed in a place where I grew smaller
Knowing I could be taller
Yet not ready to grow
Not until I had an ending we could both compre-
hend

But whatever the outcome may be
I knew I would have you in the end
To remind me of who I am
Fierce. Brilliant. Resilient.

Never Ever

Never be afraid to stand up for yourself
Never be afraid to love
Never be afraid to start over
Never be afraid to feel your emotions
Never be afraid to forgive
Never be afraid to apologize
Never be afraid to learn and grow from every experience
Ever.

Winter Solstice

I release you—

I release the guilt

I release the heartache

I release the weight I feel on my chest when I sleep

I release the soul bind we once had

I release you.

Intentions

I want to get in touch with my spirituality
I want to better my health and wellness, inside and
out
I want to focus on myself and be the best version of
me
I want to exude positive energy into the universe
I want to make my own rules up
I want to march to the beat of my own drum with no
regrets
I want to live solely for my own happiness
(But not at the expense of someone else's happiness)
I want to enjoy my own company
I want to fall in love with myself.

Final Reminder

Being in love at such a young age, through your young adult years is chaotic. The trials, tribulations, the intense emotions, the infectious love are all so beautiful but can be so ugly at the same time. Even with all the hurt, grief, and confusion that it caused me, I wouldn't take it back because it gave me perspective. Perspective on my future, my goals, my values, not only within myself but what I look for in my future partner as well.

I like to think of my first love as a karmic lesson. It taught me to deep dive within myself, to learn more about myself, to forgive myself, and to keep loving myself. My biggest blessing from all this was falling back in love with this new more gumptious version of myself and for that alone, I can forgive and move on peacefully.

Being stuck in a relationship that no longer serves a purpose to you and is no longer a healthy relationship, is not your fault. We all have different breaking points. Sometimes life isn't kind, and we don't want to leave our comfort zone. When you are ready, embrace the love from yourself, your family, friends (your support system) and find creative healthy outlets to allow yourself to heal. Healing looks different for everyone and it's not always linear. You will have good days and bad days, but you have to celebrate the good days and be kind to yourself on the bad days.

Don't empty your glass for anyone
And even if you do, don't worry
You're still half full!

Made in the USA
Monee, IL
21 November 2021